SuRVIVING

in WILD WATERS

CARLA MOONEY

Lerner Publications Company • Minneapolis

Cover photo: A yacht sinks beneath the surface of the water near Greece in 2012.

Lerner Publications Company
A division of Lerner Publishing Group, Inc.
241 First Avenue North
Minneapolis, MN 55401 USA

For reading levels and more information, look up this title at
www.lernerbooks.com.

Library of Congress Cataloging-in-Publication Data

Mooney, Carla, 1970–
    Surviving in wild waters / by Carla Mooney.
        pages   cm. — (Shockzone—True survival stories)
    Includes index.
    ISBN 978-1-4677-1436-5 (lib. bdg. : alk. paper)
    ISBN 978-1-4677-2518-7 (eBook)
    1. Survival at sea—Juvenile literature. I. Title.
  GF86.M67 2014
  910.4'52—dc23   2013024312

Manufactured in the United States of America
1 – PC – 12/31/13

TABLE OF CONTENTS

SURVIVAL AT SEA

Have you ever wondered what you would do if you were **stranded in the middle of the ocean?** This isn't just a day at the beach. What if you were hundreds of miles from land? Imagine the blazing sun beating down on you day after day. Seawater and waves in every direction. Huge storms crashing around you with no shelter in sight. And deadly sharks circling in the water, waiting for you to make a mistake. How would you handle it? Could you survive?

Many people have survived wild waters and frightening storms and lived to tell the tale. When they set out for sea, they didn't expect to have to fight for survival. Yet when incredible odds were stacked against them, each found the courage to keep going. Battling the vast ocean and the scorching sun, they found a way to make it out alive.

When boats go down at sea, stranded people are sometimes thousands of miles from any other kind of shelter.

Teens in Trouble

Three teenage cousins jumped into a 12-foot (3.7-meter) boat. It was October 2010. They had no idea the quick trip they planned would end up being a terrifying adventure. Etueni Nasau, Samuel Pelesa, and Filo Filo lived in Tokelau in the South Pacific Ocean. Tokelau is a territory of New Zealand. It is a group of three coral atolls. The teens planned to boat a short distance between two of Tokelau's islands.

atolls = tiny coral islands that consist of reefs around lagoons

During the trip, the boat's outboard motor ran out of fuel. Without a motor or paddles, the small boat began to drift out to sea. Soon, the boys were unable to see land. They sat helplessly as the boat drifted farther and farther away.

The teens grew hungrier as days went by without help. They ate a few coconuts and drank the small jar of water that they had brought on the trip. There was little else on the boat for food.

Desperate for something to eat, they turned to the sea. They ate small flying fish that jumped into the boat. Once a seagull landed on the boat. Pelesa grabbed it, and the boys ate it after drying it in the sun.

On many nights, rough seas rocked the small boat. Drenching rainstorms soaked the boys. They grabbed the sides of the heaving boat and tried to hold it upright. They feared the storms would flip the boat over. Yet the bad weather also brought fresh drinking water. Puddles of rainwater collected on the bottom of the boat. The thirsty teens lapped up the water.

Each day under the blazing tropical sun, the boys watched for any sign of a boat or land. As days turned to weeks, they saw neither. Only ocean waves surrounded them.

Catching and eating a seagull helped the boys stay alive.

Drinking seawater may seem tempting to a thirsty person, but doing so can be a deadly decision.

Meanwhile, the teens' families were sick with worry. They reported the boys missing. The Royal New Zealand Air Force searched the sea, but no sign of the tiny boat was found. The village held memorial services. Everyone was certain the teens could not have survived so long adrift at sea.

After several weeks, the teens became desperately thirsty. It had not rained for several nights. There was no rainwater to drink. They made the dangerous decision to drink seawater. Drinking seawater can be fatal. The human body cannot process the salt in seawater safely. The teens were facing certain death if they could not find freshwater soon.

A short time later, the teens spotted a boat in the distance. A deep-sea tuna boat called the *San Nikuna* was sailing to a New Zealand port. As it drew closer, the three teens waved frantically. The crew of the *San Nikuna* noticed the boys and rescued them. The teens had spent fifty days in the tiny boat. They had drifted more than 800 miles (1,300 kilometers). They were dehydrated and hungry, and they had bad sunburns. Yet they had survived.

dehydrated =
not having enough
water in the body

One of the teens called his grandmother from the tuna boat that rescued them. News of their incredible survival quickly spread through the village. Friends and family cried and hugged. They sang songs to celebrate the return of the boys.

DANGERS OF DRINKING SEAWATER

Humans need water to survive. Yet drinking seawater can be deadly. Seawater has salt. Small amounts of salt are safe for humans. But there is too much salt in seawater to drink it safely. If you drink seawater, your kidneys have to get rid of the extra salt. To do this, they produce more urine than usual. As your body produces more urine, you become dehydrated and feel thirstier. If you keep drinking seawater, you may die of dehydration.

Two of the boys are helped ashore after finally reaching land.

MT DAU

Alone at Sea

In late January 1982, Steven Callahan set sail from the tourist-filled Canary Islands off the coast of Northwest Africa. He was on a small boat he built himself. Callahan was sailing the Atlantic Ocean for the first time alone. His destination was the beautiful Caribbean island of Antigua. He planned to write a novel during the trip. Instead, disaster struck.

During the night of February 4, a large crash jolted Callahan awake. Something, possibly a whale, had hit the boat. Water began pouring into the boat's cabin. Callahan leaped from his bunk. He grabbed his survival knife and waded through the rushing water to the boat's deck. In the moonlight, Callahan could see that the boat was sinking. Wearing only a T-shirt and a diver's watch, he cut loose his nylon life raft and inflated it. He dove back into the cabin to gather survival gear. He knew he had only seconds before the boat would sink beneath the surface.

In the watery darkness of the cabin, Callahan used his hands to guide him. He grabbed a sleeping bag, a floating cushion, some cabbages and eggs, an empty coffee can, a survival manual, a spear gun, solar stills, and a radio beacon. He returned to his life raft and climbed aboard. As the heavy seas tossed him around, Callahan slowly drifted away from his sinking boat. Callahan guessed that he was hundreds of miles from land.

Callahan had only a few moments to toss survival gear into his small life raft.

Day after day passed. Thirsty, Callahan tried to set up solar stills he had grabbed from the sinking boat. The stills could turn salty seawater into fresh drinking water. With some effort, Callahan got two of them working. He also caught rainwater in a tarp. Even so, he was thirsty all the time. Callahan also caught fish to eat. As his boat drifted west, he speared and ate small fish.

Callahan tried to send a distress signal. He turned on his emergency position-indicating radio beacon. The beacon could tell people where to find him. But its signal did not reach any

SOLAR STILL

A solar still gathers saltwater through a filling tube and uses the sun to heat up the water. When the saltwater gets warm, it evaporates and turns into a gas. The salt doesn't evaporate, so it is left behind. When the gas rises, it hits a sheet of plastic or glass. The gas condenses on the plastic or glass and turns back into water. It drips through a tube into a container as drinkable, salt-free water.

PLASTIC

SEAWATER

DRINKING WATER

FILLING TUBE

Solar stills are among the most important pieces of survival gear for people stranded at sea.

on board. Forty-two days later, Ashcraft sailed the damaged yacht into Hawaii's Hilo Harbor. Thanks to her survival instincts, she had escaped her ocean ordeal alive.

ONBOARD SURVIVAL KIT

Be prepared! If you run into trouble on the water, having the right gear may be the difference between life and death. One important way to be prepared is to keep a survival kit on board. The kit should have everything you need to survive on a raft or a deserted island while waiting for rescue. A survival kit should include the following:

a compass

a flashlight

waterproof matches

a knife

sunscreen

freshwater

a mirror for signaling

flares

a first aid kit

food rations

a solar still

By the time she arrived in Hilo Harbor, Ashcraft had lost 40 pounds (18 kilograms) since she had left Tahiti.

Stranded with Sharks

In 1982 sailor Debbie Kiley boarded a 58-foot (18 m) sailing yacht in Maine. Many yachts use motors to move, but sailing yachts rely on the wind to push their sails. The twenty-four-year-old greeted the other crew members, Brad Cavanaugh, Meg Mooney, and Mark Adams. Also aboard was the skipper, John Lippoth. Together they planned a trip to deliver the yacht to Florida. None of them could have guessed that only two would survive.

Shortly after a stop in Maryland, a sudden storm rocked their boat. The yacht soon began to sink. Before it slipped below the surface, the crew managed to untie a small, inflatable lifeboat. Although they were out of the water, the group was in serious trouble. They couldn't see land. They had no way to call for help. And they were out of drinkable water. On the third night after the yacht sank, Adams and Lippoth were so thirsty they drank seawater. By the next day, they were suffering from delusions. Lippoth thought that he saw land. He jumped into the water and swam a few yards before screaming and disappearing beneath the water's surface. Adams soon jumped in the water too. He also disappeared. Kiley, Cavanaugh, and Mooney felt a thud against the boat as sharks devoured Adams.

On the raft, Mooney became extremely ill as a result of cuts she received while climbing from the yacht onto the lifeboat. Her severe injuries led to infection and blood poisoning. During the fourth night, she died. When the sun rose the next day, Kiley and Cavanaugh lifted Mooney's lifeless body over the side of the raft and let her go.

Kiley and Cavanaugh were desperate. Finally, on the fifth day after the sinking, Cavanaugh spotted a ship. The freighter drew close and crew members threw out a rope with a life ring. The freighter's crew managed to pull Kiley and Cavanaugh to safety. They were lucky to have survived the wild waters and sharks of the Atlantic Ocean.

The enormous freighter nearly drowned the survivors as it approached. Several times, its hull sucked them below the water as they attempted to get pulled aboard.

Survival in the South Atlantic

In 1942 sailor Poon Lim worked on the British merchant ship *SS Ben Lomond.* He knew his duty was dangerous, but he had no idea how soon he'd be fighting for his life. During World War II (1939–1945), British merchant ships carried supplies to troops overseas. The ships brought back food and raw materials to England. German military submarines called U-boats patrolled the Atlantic Ocean. They tried to stop the British ships from delivering their cargo. When a U-boat found a merchant ship, it attacked by firing torpedoes. The merchant ships didn't have strong defenses. Many sank after being attacked by U-boats.

On November 23, the *SS Ben Lomond* was sailing about 750 miles (1,207 km) off the coast of Brazil. Lim was in his quarters, preparing to report for duty. Suddenly, the ship lurched. Lim heard a great creaking and thrashing. Another explosion rocked the ship and knocked him off his feet. Water poured into his quarters through a broken porthole. Lim realized that two torpedoes had hit the ship.

Some men who escaped sinking ships during World War II were rescued within hours. Others—such as Lim—were not so lucky.

Prepared for emergencies such as this by weekly training drills, Lim grabbed his life jacket. He put it on as the ship leaned and shifted. Then he climbed a ladder to the deck. The ship was on fire. Black smoke filled the air. Men ran in panic around him. Lim headed for his assigned lifeboat. When he reached the spot where it should have been, he saw that the lifeboat was gone.

Without a lifeboat, Lim was forced to jump from the sinking ship into the water. He jumped overboard before the fire reached the ship's boilers and caused them to explode. He struggled to swim toward the surface. He coughed and spit saltwater. Still wearing his life jacket, he grabbed onto a piece of floating debris. Lim looked around. The ship was gone. Dead men littered the ocean surface. Of the more than fifty crew members, he was the sole survivor.

debris = pieces of something that was destroyed

Lim knew he would not survive long in the water on his own. He could barely swim. He scanned the surface for one of the ship's life rafts. After what seemed like hours, he finally spotted a square wooden raft. He slowly struggled against the waves until he reached it and climbed aboard.

In the raft, Lim found a small amount of food and water. He rationed the food and water, making it last for sixty days. Afraid that he would fall into the sea and lose the raft, Lim tied one end of a rope to the raft and the other end to his wrist. After drifting for seven days, Lim spotted a ship in the distance. It did not see him. Days later, several planes flew overhead. They too failed to see the stranded sailor. Lim lost hope. He was certain he would die at sea.

rationed = gave out in limited amounts to make something last

Thirsty, hungry, and sunburned, Lim floated alone on the raft. When his food supply ran low, Lim made a fish hook from a flashlight spring. He used rope as a fishing line and caught fish to eat. He also ate birds when he could catch them. To get water to drink, he used a tarp to collect rainwater. Lim used the remains of a bird as bait to catch a shark. When the shark bit the bait,

Lim's wooden raft was low-tech even in the 1940s, when advanced inflatable life rafts like the one shown here were available.

Lim yanked on the line, pulling the shark onto the raft. There, he beat the shark to death with a water jug. To pass the time, Lim sang folk songs. He used the position of the moon to track the time during the night. He counted full moons as the days, weeks, and months passed.

Eventually, Lim's raft floated near land. A fishing crew from Brazil spotted him and brought him to the port city of Belém. After an incredible 133 days floating in the South Atlantic Ocean, Lim walked off the raft without help.

After his rescue, Lim became world famous.

FOUR MONTHS ADRIFT

In May 2002, sixty-two-year-old Richard Van Pham set out on a sailing trip from his home in Long Beach, California, to Catalina Island. He expected the 22-mile (35 km) trip to take about three hours. He had no idea a frightening three-month journey lay ahead. On the way to the island, a sudden storm struck. The whipping winds broke the sailboat's mast and wrecked his motor. Pham had no way to power the boat. He had no radio, so there was no way to contact anyone for help. He had no close family and had not filed a float plan. When he did not arrive in Catalina, no one reported him missing. A rescue search was never launched.

Without a sail or a motor, Pham's 26-foot (8 m) sailboat drifted in the ocean. The winds and ocean currents pushed him steadily south. During the day, Pham spent most of his time below deck to stay out of the sun. He collected rainwater to drink in a 5-gallon (19-liter) bucket. He caught and ate fish from the sea. Sometimes, he hooked fish to his broken mast to lure seabirds. He made a makeshift grill from the boat's wood paneling to cook the birds he caught. He even landed a sea turtle and salted its meat to save for times when food was low.

Every day, Pham scanned the horizon for a ship or a plane. Day after day, he saw nothing. He slept and drifted alone. Finally, on September 17, 2002, Pham spotted a plane. It tipped its wings to signal that it had seen him. Pham knew that help was on its way.

Pham was spotted by a US government P-3 Orion airplane that had been searching for drug smugglers.

Meanwhile, a US Navy ship named the *McClusky* was traveling along the west coast of Central America. It received a report from the airplane that a broken-down sailboat was nearby. The *McClusky* sailed toward the area. Less than two hours later, the ship's crew spotted the sailboat. Pham's boat had floated 2,500 miles (4,000 km) since it was disabled in the storm. It was now off the Pacific coast of Costa Rica.

When the *McClusky* blew its whistle, Pham appeared on the sailboat's deck and waved his arms. The ship lowered a boat into the water with sailors and a medic. When they reached Pham's boat, he was in the middle of making a lunch of roasted seabird on his makeshift grill.

medic =
someone trained
to give medical
help in an
emergency

The *McClusky* had a history of rescuing people. It participated in an evacuation from a volcano in 1991.

Pham was happy to see the sailors. Yet he did not want to leave his boat. Instead, he asked the sailors to help him fix his mast. He also needed a new sail. He believed he was still near Catalina, and he refused medical treatment. After four months at sea, Pham planned to keep sailing. The *McClusky* sailors told Pham that his broken-down boat would not be able to sail. It was simply unsafe. This finally convinced Pham to abandon his boat.

When the *McClusky* was unable to tow the sailboat, Pham gave the US Navy permission to sink it. After almost four months at sea, Pham had lost some weight. But a medical exam showed that otherwise he was remarkably healthy. The ship dropped Pham off in Guatemala. With money donated by the crew of the *McClusky*, the sailing survivor purchased a ticket for a flight back to the United States.

FLOAT PLAN

If you plan to sail for more than a few hours, you should leave a written copy of a float plan with your local marina or a friend. A float plan describes your boat and safety equipment. It lists the people on board. It also details where you are going and when you expect to arrive. When you arrive safely, notify the person holding your float plan. If you do not arrive within a reasonable time, the person holding your float plan should notify the Coast Guard or other rescue agency.

Sailors from the *McClusky* had to board Pham's boat to convince him to leave.

10 Boating Safety Tips

According to the US Coast Guard, there are more than 12 million recreational boats registered in the United States. With so many boaters on the water, accidents will happen. To prevent accidents and stay safe on the water, here are 10 important boating safety tips:

1. Everyone on board should wear a life jacket at all times.

2. Never drink alcohol while operating a boat.

3. Take a boating safety course to learn the rules of the water.

4. Understand and obey boating and navigational rules every time you are on the water.

6. Keep an eye out for other boaters to prevent collisions or other accidents.

7. Check the weather forecast before you head out on the water.

8. Carry an emergency position-indicating radio beacon or similar device. If you get lost or stranded, it will help rescuers find you quickly.

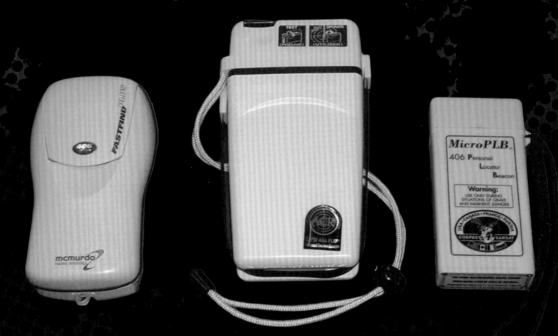

9. Use a carbon monoxide detector on board. It will warn you if the deadly gas is building up inside the boat's cabin.

10. File a float plan before you set sail. That way, if you encounter trouble, rescuers will be better prepared to find you.

Boating Safety Resource Center
http://www.uscgboating.org/
If you're planning on going boating, be sure to go here first for tons of safety tips. Find safety stats, cool videos, and information about the laws of the sea on this helpful site run by the US Coast Guard.

Ocean
http://ocean.nationalgeographic.com/ocean/
Learn everything you ever wanted to know about the ocean on this cool site. Check out photo galleries, maps, and quizzes. You can even learn about modern-day pirates!

Park, Louise. *The Sinking of the Titanic.* Discovery Education: Sensational True Stories series. New York: PowerKids Press, 2013.
After the *Titanic* sank in 1912, thousands of passengers fought for survival in chilly waters until help arrived. Read this book to learn more about this amazing survival story.

Solar Still
http://pbskids.org/zoom/activities/sci/solarstill.html
Test your ocean survival skills by making your own solar still! This site has step-by-step instructions on how to create one of these handy survival tools.

Stewart, Melissa. *Is the Bermuda Triangle Really a Dangerous Place? And Other Questions about the Ocean.* Minneapolis: Lerner Publications, 2011.
In this book, you'll discover little-known facts about the ocean and the creatures that live in it.

PHOTO ACKNOWLEDGMENTS

The images in this book are used with the permission of: © McCarthy's PhotoWorks/Shutterstock Images, p. 4; © Joel Calheiros/Shutterstock Images, p. 5; © R McIntyre/Shutterstock Images, p. 6; © Brian Lasenby/ Shutterstock Images, p. 7; © Elenamiv/Shutterstock Images, p. 8; © Pita Ligaiula/AP Images, p. 9; © slava296/Shutterstock Images, p. 10; © David Wingate/Shutterstock Images, p. 11; © Darren Anaum/DK Images, p. 12; © Pat Wellenbach/AP Images, p. 13; © Anton Balazh/Shutterstock Images, p. 14; © John Lund/SuperStock, p. 15; © BlueGreen Pictures/SuperStock, p. 16; © cecoffman/Shutterstock Images, p. 17; © Peter Franke/Mauritius/ SuperStock, p. 18; © Sascha Burkard/Shutterstock Images, p. 19; © Bettmann/Corbis/AP Images, p. 20; © AP Images, pp. 21, 22, 23; © Corky Buczyk/Shutterstock Images, p. 24; US Navy, p. 25; Michael D. Kennedy/US Navy, p. 26; © US Navy/AP Images, p. 27; US Coast Guard, p. 28; NOAA, p. 29.

Front Cover: AP Photo/Greek Navy, HO.

Main body text set in Calvert MT Std Regular 11/16.
Typeface provided by Monotype Typography.